JOHN THOMPSON'S MODERN COURSE
FOR THE PIANO

TEACHING LITTLE FINGERS TO PLAY

PLAYBACK+
Speed • Pitch • Balance • Loop

To access audio, visit:
www.halleonard.com/mylibrary

Enter Code
8873-0292-4717-4878

Cover, Design, and Illustrations by Nicholas E. Gressle © 1994, 2017

ISBN 978-1-4584-1968-2

WILLIS MUSIC

EXCLUSIVELY DISTRIBUTED BY

HAL•LEONARD®

Visit Hal Leonard Online at
www.halleonard.com

Contact us:
Hal Leonard
7777 West Bluemound Road
Milwaukee, WI 53213
Email: info@halleonard.com

In Europe, contact:
Hal Leonard Europe Limited
42 Wigmore Street
Marylebone, London, W1U 2RN
Email: info@halleonardeurope.com

In Australia, contact:
Hal Leonard Australia Pty. Ltd.
4 Lentara Court
Cheltenham, Victoria, 3192 Australia
Email: info@halleonard.com.au

TO THE TEACHER
HOW TO PRESENT THE FIRST THREE LESSONS IN *TEACHING LITTLE FINGERS TO PLAY*

When children can place their tiny fingers on the piano keyboard and PLAY A TUNE during the first few moments of their first lesson they discover that to learn music is as easy as any play-time activity. Hence, the advisability of TEACHING BY ROTE.

This book incorporates rote teaching, the ADVANTAGE of this being that the pupil cheerfully makes music while simultaneously mastering the necessary rudiments required to PLAY BY NOTE.

The following procedure, if carefully observed, will teach any pupil to MAKE MUSIC FIVE MINUTES after the first lesson, and by the fourth lesson the pupil will be able to PLAY BY NOTE.

FIRST LESSON

The musical examples in the first three lessons are to be taught ENTIRELY BY ROTE (i.e., imitation). The purpose is to teach the NAMES OF THE KEYS ONLY. The notes will be learned later.

1. Teach *Stepping* and *Skipping*, first as a song. The teacher plays and sings a few times until the pupil memorizes both TUNE and WORDS. (The pupil is already making music.)
When the pupil can SING it correctly, teach him to PLAY it on the piano by *finger patterns*.

2. Teach the *number names* of the fingers.

Left Hand   Right Hand

3. Teacher PLAYS and SINGS the *first pattern* slowly using the number names of the fingers thus:

FIRST PATTERN

SING: ONE   TWO   THREE

SECOND PATTERN

SING: THREE   TWO   ONE

4. When the pupil can *imitate* the first pattern, PLAY and SING the second pattern the same way and have the pupil imitate.

5. Now PLAY and SING the *third pattern* and have the pupil imitate in exactly the same way.

THIRD PATTERN

SING: TWO   THREE   ONE

6. When the pupil can play all three patterns using the number names of the fingers, then teach him or her to play and sing the *letter names of the keys*:

SING: C   D   E   E   D   C   D   E   C

PLAY:

7. After the pupil has played the three patterns, first with the RIGHT HAND and then with the LEFT HAND ALONE, he or she should be instructed to play them in different octaves on the keyboard; see example below.

RIGHT HAND
SING: C   D   E   E   D   C   D   E   C

LEFT HAND
SING: C   D   E   E   D   C   D   E   C

TO THE TEACHER (Continued)

The pupil has sung and played a tune in much less time than it has taken to describe. He or she has played with the LEFT and RIGHT hands and developed the first three fingers of each hand equally.

THE PUPIL HAS LEARNED TO RECOGNIZE AND PLAY THREE KEYS ON THE KEYBOARD

THE LESSON IN NOTATION

The first lesson is very simple. The pupil is taught to recognize the TREBLE and BASS CLEF signs, BAR LINES and MEASURES as illustrated on page 5. Teachers usually have individual methods for teaching the rudiments; hence, all examples are subject to the effect of a suggestion — the success of your own individuality.

SECOND LESSON

Proceed exactly as in Lesson One. First as a SONG, then by FINGER PATTERNS (*pupil singing number names of fingers*). Finally as shown in example (*pupil now singing letter names of keys*).

After the pupil can play the example with each hand separately in various octaves COMBINE GROUPS 2 and 1 as follows:

SING:

The pupil has learned FIVE keys on the keyboard — A B C D E — and can PLAY and SING a tune of 8 measures, using both hands.

THE LESSON IN NOTATION

In this second lesson, the pupil is taught to recognize and know the value of QUARTER-NOTES, HALF- and WHOLE - NOTES.

(The quarter - note is used as a unit instead of the whole - note to avoid fractions. "ONE NOTE, ONE COUNT," is easily understood, whereas when the whole - note is taught first, the child is asked to *divide a note in his* mind into four fractional parts.)

THIRD LESSON

Teach the remaining letter - names E F G by presenting Stepping and Skipping on the new keys as in other lessons.

When the example can be played with either hand in various octaves COMBINE GROUPS 3 and 1 as follows:

The pupil now learns TIME SIGNATURES in the LESSON IN NOTATION (pg. 7).

He has learned all 7 white keys — A B C D E F G, has been making music for three lessons and has absorbed enough knowledge of NOTATION to enable him or her to read without dictation from now on. Thus ROTE TEACHING has been used as a MEANS TOWARD AN END.

(NOTE: — After the third lesson, material should be assigned according to the capacity of each individual pupil)

Contents

"Something New Every Lesson"

To the Teacher...2

First Keyboard and Notation Lesson *(Rote)*.........5

Second Keyboard and Notation Lesson *(Rote)*......6

Third Keyboard and Notation Lesson *(Rote)*.........7

Correlating Keys and Notes *(C,D,E)* —
    "The Birthday Party"...8

Correlating Keys and Notes *(A,B,C)* —
    "Sandman's Near"..9

Two Notes in Both Directions from Middle C *(2/4) time)* —
    "Baseball Days"...10

Three Notes in Both Directions from Middle C
    (Dotted half-note 3/4 time) — "The Postman" 11

Four - Four Time —
    "Rain on the Roof"..12

Dotted Half-note in 4/4 Time *(A minor)* —
    "Song of the Volga Boatmen" 13

Musical Sentences called Phrases —
    "A Message"...14

Four Notes in Both Directions from Middle C—
    "Chimes"...15

The Tale of a Famous Carol —
    "Good King Wenceslas".......................................16

Signs of Silence called Rests —
    "Lazy Mary"..17

Cross-Hand —
    "Betty and Bill"..18

Time Value of Eighth Notes —
    "Flying to the Moon"...19

Skipping a White Key *(3rd's)* —
    "Air, from Surprise Symphony" 20

Introducing Bass Notes C and G *(an octave below Middle C)* —
    "By the Pond"...21

The Black Key Sign called Sharp —
    "Paper Ships"...22

F Sharp in the Key Signature —
    "Sledding"...23

Second Recreation in the Key of G *(the Tie)*
    "The Butterfly"...24

Introducing Treble Notes *(an octave above Middle C)* —
    "Questions"...25

Middle C Sharp *(Accidental)* —
    "Blue Bells of Scotland" 26

Skipping White Keys *(Triad)* —
    "Toy Soldiers"...27

A Few Measures with Two Hands Together —
    "Big Ships"..28

The Flat and Accidental Signs —
    "Steamboat 'round the Bend" 29

B♭ in the Key Signature —
    "Comin Round the Mountain" *(Duet)* 30-31

Cross-Hand —
    "The Long Trail"...32

An Accidental *(A sharp)* —
    "The Bee"..33

Beginning on a Weak Beat —
    "My Bonnie"...34

Using the 8--- Sign —
    "Vacation Time"..35

Expression —
    "Home on the Range" *(Duet)*.........................36-37

Cross-hand — R.H. and L.H. —
    "The Juggler"...38

Two Notes Together *(Chord)* —
    "From a Wigwam" 39

Certificate of Merit..40

Teachers who, for the sake of thoroughness, desire to have the pupil practice writing BAR LINES, CLEFS, TIME SIGNATURES, etc., etc., will find "JOHN THOMPSON'S NOTE SPELLER" very useful. — J.T.

FIRST LESSON AT THE KEYBOARD
LEARNING THE KEYS **C D E**

The **BLACK** keys of the piano keyboard are divided into patterns of **TWO** and **THREE**. To the left of the TWO **BLACK** key pattern, in the center of your piano under the maker's name, is **MIDDLE C.**

Locate, and play MIDDLE C
with the FIRST finger (*THUMB*) of your RIGHT hand.

MIDDLE C D E

D is between

To the RIGHT of the
TWO BLACK key pattern is E

LEFT HAND

RIGHT HAND

Stepping and Skipping

Step-ping up, Step-ping down, Then a skip.

(1) Learn first as a SONG. **(2)** PLAY and SING the words. **(3)** Play and sing the letter-names of the KEYS. **(4)** Play each hand separately in VARIOUS OCTAVES.

FIRST LESSON IN NOTATION
Learning the Grand Staff, Clef Signs, Bars and Measures

TREBLE CLEF
SIGN

BASS CLEF

BAR LINE   BAR LINE   BAR LINE   DOUBLE BAR LINE

←— MEASURE —→ ←— MEASURE —→ ←— MEASURE —→ ←— MEASURE —→

Always placed at the
end of a piece
of music.

SECOND LESSON AT THE KEYBOARD

NEW KEYS A, B, and playing A, B, C

MIDDLE

A B C

B's neighbor is A

To the RIGHT of the three BLACK
Key pattern is B

Always
Be
Curious

to find other A, B, C's
on the keyboard.

Stepping and Skipping from A

Step - ping up,   Step-ping down, Then   a   skip.

Combining Group 2 and Group 1

GROUP 1

GROUP 2

SECOND LESSON IN NOTATION:
Notes, like Coins, have different values.

A QUARTER NOTE
IS HELD FOR
1 COUNT

A HALF NOTE
IS HELD FOR
2 COUNTS

A WHOLE NOTE
IS HELD FOR
4 COUNTS

THIRD LESSON AT THE KEYBOARD

NEW KEYS F, G, and playing E, F, G

MIDDLE C

F G

To the LEFT of the three BLACK Key pattern is F

F's neighbor is G

Always
Be
Curious
to find other E, F, G's on the keyboard.

Stepping and Skipping from E

1　2　3　　3　2　1　　2　3　　　1

3　2　1　　1　2　3　　2　1　　3

Step-ping up,　Step-ping down, Then　a　skip.

Combining Group 3 and 1

GROUP 3 - Play with right hand

1　2　3

3　2　1

GROUP 1 - Play with left hand

THIRD LESSON IN NOTATION

The TIME SIGNATURE next to the CLEF sign at the beginning of a piece tells us how it should be counted.

Upper figure means that there are two counts to a measure.

Count: 1　2　　1　2

Lower figure means that each quarter note gets one count.

THREE Counts to a measure.

Count: 1　2　3　　1 2 3

Quarter Note gets one count.

FOUR counts to a measure.

Count: 1　2　3　4　　1 2 3 4　1234

Quarter Note gets one count.

Birthday Party

Right hand **GROUP** for this piece.
Locate C D E in other parts
of keyboard.

1-3

| Strong beat | Weak beat | | | |
| Here | we | go, | Up a | row, |

| To | a | birth - day | par - | ty. |

Left hand GROUP for this piece. Locate and play A B C in other parts of the keyboard.

4-6 # Sandman's Near

Dol - ly dear, Sand-man's near,

You will soon be sleep - ing.

Baseball Days

7-9

Come on kids, join the fun,

Base - ball days have be - gun.

When the stem of Middle C goes Up, play it with the right hand.
When the stem of Middle C goes Down, play it with the left hand.

Upper figure means that there are 3 counts in each measure.

Lower figure means that each quarter note gets one count.

THE DOTTED HALF-NOTE
(THREE-BEAT NOTE)

HOLD 3 BEATS (1, 2, 3).
A DOT after a note increases its value by half of its original value.

The Postman

10-12

STRONG   WEAK   WEAK

Post-man I'll be when I grow tall;

Let-ters I'll bring you in win-ter and fall.

In ¾ Time, be sure to accent the first beat of each measure.

The Dotted Half-Note ♩. **In 4/4 Time.**

🔊 16-18

Song of the Volga Boatmen

Yo, yo, heave | ho! Oh, yo, yo, heave | ho! So

pull to - | geth - er; | for - ward still we | go.

Music is written in HAPPY KEYS (*Major*) and SAD keys (*Minor*).

This famous Russian Folk-Song is an example in a SAD key.

Years ago, before there were steamboats, the peasants who lived along the banks of the Volga used to pull boats and barges, heavily loaded with merchandise, up the river from one village to the next.

The plodding along the banks of those condemned to this labor was terrible. While struggling along they used to lighten their burden by singing the sad strains of this rhythmical melody.

Groups of notes, like words in books,
tell stories when arranged in sentences
and punctuated.
A curved line over groups of notes indicates
MUSICAL SENTENCES called PHRASES.

L.H. Group   R.H. Group

A Message

19-21

English Folk-Tune

Tap, tap, tap, tap, | someone's knock-ing | at my door to | bring a let- ter;

Tap, tap, tap, tap, | I wish they'd ring; | Our bell sounds much | bet- ter.

L.H. Group   R.H. Group

22-24

Chimes

Ding dong, dong ding | Hear the chimes ring; | From the high tow'r,

Hark to the hour. | ONE | TWO | THREE | FOUR.

Good King Wenceslas

This very ancient tune was a great favorite among the carol singers who used to beg for alms many centuries ago. It is based on the legend of King Wenceslas the Holy, who was king of Bohemia in the Tenth Century. On the Feast of St. Stephen (Dec. 26), this good king went out among the poor and gave liberally.

25-27

English Christmas Carol

In music notation there are signs of silence, called **RESTS**, which tell us when and how many beats our fingers should be silent.

	QUARTER REST	HALF REST	WHOLE * REST
Pictures of RESTS	𝄽	▬	▬
Relative Note Value	♩	𝅗𝅥	𝅝
Beats (Count)	1	1, 2	1, 2, 3, 4

*The whole rest covers the whole measure, regardless of the time signature.

Lazy Mary

28-30

READ and name the four notes above and three notes below MIDDLE C. Count as you play.

18

Betty and Bill

31-33

Gal - lop - ing, gal - lop - ing o - ver the hill,

O, what a frol - ic for *L.H.* Bet - ty and Bill.

Flying to the Moon

34-36

American Folk Tune
(Adapted)

Shall we go a - fly - ing, fly - ing, fly - ing?

Shall we go a - fly - ing to the moon?

The time value of an eighth note ♪ is HALF as long as that of a quarter note.

Play TWO eighth notes ♫ to ONE count.

"PAPA HAYDN", as Mozart lovingly called this great musician, inherited his sense of humor from his father, Mathias Haydn, who was a hard-working and jolly man. He lived in Rohrau, a small Austrian village where, in a combination shop and home, he made and repaired wheels. He had a fine tenor voice and was the sexton and organist in the village church. His wife sang in the choir.

Young Joseph had eleven brothers and sisters. At the age of 5 he was taken to a nearby village where he was taught music. He was always full of mischief and one day, as a result of a prank, he was turned out into the stormy night—homeless.

The following morning, he went to a friend, a wigmaker and barber, who let him use his garret. Here, on a dilapidated harpsichord, with snow blowing through the cracks of the roof, Joseph worked and studied.

On moonlit nights he and his friends used to stroll about the streets of Vienna serenading famous musicians. After years of hard work, he wrote some of the most magnificent compositions known.

L.H. Group
Skipping 1 WHITE KEY

R.H. Group
Skipping 2 WHITE KEYS

37-39

Air
(from Surprise Symphony)

Pa - pa Hay -dn's dead and gone, But his mem'- ry lin -gers on;

When his mood was one of bliss, He wrote jol - ly tunes like this.

🔊 **40-42**

By the Pond

"Quack", "quack", "quack!" goes the fun - ny duck,

"Croak", "croak", "croak!" goes the frog - gie too.

Always
Be
Curious

to find other F♯
BLACK keys on the piano.

L.H. Group   R.H. Group - Note BLACK KEY

This sign ♯ is called a SHARP. In this piece you will see it in the first and fifth measures in front of F.
It means to play the BLACK key to the right of F instead of the white key F.

Paper Ships

43-45

When I launch my   pa - per ships in   moth - er's shin - y   pail,   Ah,

How I wish I   were a cap - tain   real - ly un - der   sail.

Sledding

46-48

When the SHARP sign ♯ is placed between the Clef sign and the time signature it becomes the KEY Signature. In this piece ALL F's must be sharped—*played on BLACK key F.*

Snow - flakes fall - ing fluff - y and white;

O, what fun! We're sled - ding to - night.

NOTE: This piece contains the Scale of G Major. Those who desire to introduce scales at this stage of instruction may have their students make good use of *Peter's Blank Music Book* (wide ruling).

24

PREPARATION
Locate, name and play the L.H. Group and then the R.H. Group.

L.H. Group

R.H. Group

52-54

Questions

Dwarf

1   2

"Gi - ant,   why   are   you   so   tall?"

Giant

"Well,   sir,   why   are   you   so   small?"

3   2

55-57

Blue Bells of Scotland

C♯ (Sharp)
Look and listen for Black Middle C

O where, and O where is your High-land lad-die gone? O where, and O

where is your High-land lad-die gone? He's gone to fight the foe for King

George up-on the throne; And it's Oh! in my heart, I wish him safe at home!

L.H. Group
Skipping 2 LINE NOTES

R.H. Group
Skipping 2 SPACE NOTES

58-60

Toy Soldiers

Sol - diers in   blue,   Sol - diers in   red,   Stag - ing a   bat - tle,   here   on   my   bed.

Line   up   the   rank,   Charge on the   flank,   On - ward, brave   sol - diers!   go where you're   led.

Big Ships

61-63

I see the big ships a - sail - ing

O - ver the pret - ty blue sea, I'd like to know where they're

go - ing, But they will nev - er tell me.

Always **B**e **C**urious

to look and listen for the
FLAT, SHARP, and NATURAL.

This is the sign called FLAT: ♭
It means that you must play the
first BLACK key to the LEFT of
the white key A in this piece.

This sign is a NATURAL: ♮
It means that when you see it
in front of a note that has just
been played on a black key, you
must now play it on its NATURAL,
the white key.

Steamboat Round the Bend

64-66

Comin' Round the Mountain

SECONDO

(For Teacher or Slightly Advanced Pupil)

Comin' Round the Mountain

67-69

PRIMO

Southern Mountain Song

As lively as possible

B♭ in the key signature means that you must play all B's on the BLACK key to the LEFT of the white key B.

Repeat ad lib.

70-72

The Long Trail

Hik- ing the trails of the Rock - ies,

lots of fun.

Climb-ing up hill ver - y slow - ly, come down on the run.

L.H. Group   R.H. Group

"A" SHARP is the first BLACK KEY to the Right of A

Skipping SPACE notes F and A

73-75

The Bee

Buzz - ing, buzz - ing, buzz - ing, buzz - ing bee in the grass,

Please to be po - lite e - nough to let me pass.

This piece begins on a weak beat—the last count in a measure. You must therefore ACCENT the first beat after the bar line. The missing counts of the first measure will be found in the last measure of the piece.

76-78

My Bonnie

8----- means: Play EIGHT keys higher

Vacation Time

I'm waltz - ing a - round in a mer - ry mood, I'm hav - ing a great deal of

fun, There's nev - er a cloud in the sky to - day, Va -

ca - tion has be - gun.

Home on the Range

SECONDO

Slowly, with much expression

Teacher or slightly advanced pupil

Cowboy Ballad

Home on the Range

PRIMO

Slowly, with much expression

Cowboy Ballad

D.S. al Fine—go back to the % sign and play until the **Fine.**

The Juggler

85-87

Play both
keys together

R.H. Group.

E♭ is the 1st BLACK key to the LEFT of E.

88-90

From a Wigwam

CERTIFICATE of MERIT

This certifies that

···

has successfully completed

TEACHING LITTLE FINGERS TO PLAY

and is eligible for promotion to

"TEACHING LITTLE FINGERS TO PLAY MORE"

···
Teacher

···
Date

Cut certificate out on dotted line.